The Culture of the QIN and HAN Dynasties of China

Vic Kovacs

PowerKiDS press.

NEW YORK

Published in 2017 by **The Rosen Publishing Group, Inc.**
29 East 21ˢᵗ Street, New York, NY 10010

Cataloging-in-Publication Data

Names: Kovacs, Vic.
Title: The culture of the Qin and Han dynasties of China / Vic Kovacs.
Description: New York : PowerKids Press, 2017. | Series: Ancient cultures and civilizations | Includes index.
Identifiers: ISBN 9781508150084 (pbk.) | ISBN 9781508150039 (library bound) | ISBN 9781508149941 (6 pack)
Subjects: LCSH: China--History--To 221 B.C.--Juvenile literature. | China--History--Qin dynasty, 221-207 B.C.--
    Juvenile literature. | China--History--Han dynasty, 202 B.C.-220 A.D.--Juvenile literature.
Classification: LCC DS741.5 K68 2017 | DDC 931--dc23

Developed and produced for Rosen by BlueAppleWorks Inc.

Art Director: Haley Harasymiw
Managing Editor for BlueAppleWorks: Melissa McClellan
Editors: Janice Dyer, Marcia Abramson
Design: T.J. Choleva

Picture credits: p. 5 feiyuezhangjie/Shutterstock; p. 7, 17, 19, 23, 23 inset 28 Public Domain; p. 9 Mike Fisher/
Creative Commons; p. 9 right cl2004lhy/Shutterstock; p. 10 inset Alexander Vershinin/Shutterstock; p. 10 Zhao
jian kang /Shutterstock; p. 13 fotohunter/Shutterstock; p. 18 bottom right, 18 top right Vassil/Public Domain;
p. 18 bottom left Rowanwindwhistler/Creative Commons; p. 18 bottom middle Refrain/Creative Commons;
p. 18 Yeung Ping Shen Creative Commons; p. 24 Giuseppe Castiglione/Public Domain; p. 25 Rueangrit Srisuk/
Shutterstock; p. 25 inset konstantin32/Shutterstock; p. 27 Dennis Jarvis/Creative Commons; p. 29 inset
robinimages2013/Shutterstock; p. 29 maoyunping/Shutterstock; Maps: p. 8 T.J. Choleva; p. 14 T.J. Choleva.

Manufactured in the United States of America
CPSIA Compliance Information: Batch #BS16PK: For Further Information contact Rosen Publishing, New York, New York at 1-800-237-9932

CONTENTS

CHAPTER 1

UNIFIED CHINA

People were living in China over a million years ago. The first known government was the Xia **Dynasty**, which ruled from approximately 2070 B.C. They were replaced by the Shang Dynasty around 1600 B.C. They kept power for over 500 years, until 1046 B.C. After them came the Zhou Dynasty, which was the longest lasting Chinese dynasty in history. Their reign lasted until about 256 B.C. During much of that time, though, they were steadily losing power. Even though there was technically a Zhou king during most of this era, he held almost no actual power. Instead, seven rival states fought among themselves.

These wars ended in 221 B.C. when the king of the state of Qin, Ying Zheng, conquered the other six states. This effectively united China. Zheng then crowned himself the first emperor, or huang, of China. This title continued to be used by Chinese rulers for 2,000 years.

Although the Qin Dynasty had successfully united the country, it soon became known for its brutality. As a result, it did not survive for long. After a period of **civil war**, the Han Dynasty emerged in 202 B.C. It lasted for 400 years, and formed the foundation that Chinese life and culture was built on for centuries.

The Great Wall of China is the longest wall in the world. During the Qin Dynasty, the wall was built to prevent invasion from northern nations. In the Han Dynasty, the wall was extended into today's western China to protect trading routes.

CHAPTER 2

THE QIN DYNASTY

In Chinese history, the era between 475 and 221 B.C. is known as the Warring States Period. During that time, the seven states all fought for territory and control. The dominant state to emerge in this time was Qin, in the west of the country. The other states involved were Han, Wei, Zhao, Chu, Yan, and Qi. The Warring States Period was a bloody time in China. The Battle of Changping, between the Qin and Zhao, resulted in 500,000 deaths alone.

In 246 B.C., Ying Zheng became king of Qin after the death of his father. He was only thirteen years old at the time. In 230 B.C., King Zheng conquered the state of Han. Over the next nine years, his armies conquered the rest of the warring states. He was the first king of Qin to achieve this goal. This was also the first time all of China had been unified since the height of the Zhou Dynasty's power. After uniting China, Ying Zheng created the title of huang, meaning emperor. He then changed his name to Qin Shi Huang, which translates to First Emperor.

CHINESE NAMES

In Chinese, family names come first, and given names come last. For example, John Smith in America would be Smith John in China. This is true in other Asian languages as well, such as Japanese.

Qin Shi Huang named the unified empire after his kingdom Qin. Qin is pronounced as Chin. Some historians believe that this is the origin of the Western word China.

A united China led to many changes within society. With a unified country came a central unified government. Territories and states were no longer ruled over by **feudal** lords and kings. A complex **bureaucracy** was created, with the emperor as its supreme authority. As a result of having one central government, the entire country also shared the same laws. For example, something that may have been legal in one state but illegal in another was now legal throughout the country. The city of Xianyang was made the capital of united China. The philosophy that governed the Qin Dynasty was Legalism. Legalism focused on strict, clear laws that were equally applied to everyone.

The Qin Dynasty also standardized many other things that had previously been different all over the country. Written language was made the same throughout China. This allowed people from different parts of the country to communicate with each other more easily.

■ The Qin Empire

Russia

Kazakhstan

Mongolia

North Korea

South Korea

Kyrgyzstan

Tajikistan

Afghanistan

China

Pakistan

Nepal

Bhutan

India

Burma

Vietnam

Laos

This replica of the Emperor Qin Shi Huang throne shows the splendor of early rulers of China.

A standard for weights and measures was also created, which meant that the same quantities of goods were being sold for the same amount everywhere. The Ban Liang, a round coin with a square cut out of the middle, was made the standard coin during the Qin Dynasty. This allowed people to set standard prices all over the country. The state also became the only producer of coins. This eliminated private **mints**, which cut down on confusion about how much different coins were worth.

Shi Huang created the Great Wall of China. The emperor connected and extended the old walls along the north of China that originated about 700 B.C. The new wall stretched farther than any previous **fortification**. To this day, it is one of the largest construction projects ever.

THE QIN DYNASTY ENDS

Shi Huang and the Qin Dynasty introduced many important changes to China. Despite this, he was not well loved by his people. The laws and government were known to be very harsh, especially when it came to punishments. Taxes for citizens were also very high.

Education and free thought were frowned upon during his reign. The emperor believed that subjects with less education were easier to control. This led to the destruction and burning of many books that discussed philosophies other than Legalism. As a result, many of these works have been lost forever. Many scholars and **intellectuals** were killed, as well. According to ancient histories, there was even an event in which 460 scholars were ordered buried alive.

Qin Shi Huang had thousands of life-size figures of warriors and horses built as part of his **mausoleum**. They are arranged in battle formation. Tourists can see the figures at a popular museum in China.

TERRACOTTA ARMY

The Terracotta Army is one of Shi Huang's most impressive accomplishments. It is a massive collection of life-sized statues that were built to guard the emperor in the afterlife. It is based on the Qin army that finally conquered the rest of China and ended the Warring States Period. The army is made up of thousands of life-size sculptures of warriors, horses, and chariots. They are all arranged in battle formation, just like a real army. The warriors even have unique faces!
One of the most impressive aspects of the Terracotta Army, other than its size, is how long it remained hidden. The statues weren't found until 1974, over two thousand years after the death of Shi Huang. They are placed to the east of his tomb, guarding his final resting place. Their construction took 700,000 workers, another of Shi Huang's ambitious building projects.

Many people were also forced into hard labor, to work on the emperor's construction projects. These included the Great Wall and expansions of roads and canals.

In 210 B.C., Shi Huang was traveling throughout China. The purpose of his tour was said to be to inspect different regions of his empire. However, there is evidence to suggest that he was actually looking for the **elixir** of life, which was said to make a person **immortal**. It's well known that the emperor had become almost obsessed with this search, due to his growing fear of death. However, his search failed, and he died on September 10 of that year. Without his leadership, the Qin Dynasty fell just a few years later.

11

CHAPTER 3

THE HAN DYNASTY COMES TO POWER

After the death of Shi Huang, two of his advisers wanted to place his son, Hu Hai, on the throne. They believed Hu Hai, who took the name Qin Er Shi, was weak, and would be easy to control. Due to his poor leadership, revolts and civil war soon broke out. One of Qin Er Shi's advisers forced him to commit suicide and replaced him with Ziying. Ziying's rule lasted less than fifty days. The Qin Dynasty collapsed not long after.

GENERAL LIU BANG

Liu Bang was a rebel who fought against the Qin Dynasty. In fact, the last Qin emperor, Ziying, surrendered to him. He was declared the king of Han in 206 B.C. Han was one of eighteen kingdoms that the Qin empire had been split into. Liu Bang then battled a general, Xiang Yu, for control of China. Emerging victorious in 202 B.C., Liu Bang established the Han Dynasty, which reunified China. It would last for over 400 years. Liu Bang would go down in history as the first emperor to start life as a **peasant**.

NEW DYNASTY, NEW RULES

Liu Bang kept many of the **innovations** that the Qin Dynasty had made. These included a strong, central government with the emperor as its leader. He also kept the massive bureaucracy that supported the government.

In Chinese **mythology** the dragon is a symbol of power, strength, and good fortune. The emperors of China used the dragon as a symbol of their imperial power.

13

However, many of the less popular aspects of the Qin regime were abandoned. Taxes were lowered during Bang's reign. Bang also felt he was responsible for making sure the people had what they needed. Perhaps because he was born a peasant, he did not build new palaces or buildings, although he continued work on the Great Wall. Bang believed that good government means good people.

Liu Bang was a much gentler ruler than Shi Huang had ever been. He did not rule through fear. Laws were made more reasonable. Punishments, when those laws were broken, were generally much less severe than they had been under Qin rule. For a while, Legalism remained the dominant philosophy. This was mostly due to the destruction of books containing other philosophies during the Qin Dynasty.

■ The Han Empire
□ Great Wall of China

Russia
Kazakhstan
Mongolia
North Korea
Kyrgyzstan
Tajikistan
South Korea
Afghanistan
China
Pakistan
Nepal
Bhutan
India
Burma
Vietnam
Laos

CONFUCIANISM

Confucianism is a philosophy based on the teachings of the Chinese philosopher Confucius. Confucius lived from 551 to 479 B.C. The philosophy was developed during a time in Chinese history known as the Spring and Autumn Period. This was a time of instability that came before the Warring States Period. Considered by some to be a religion, Confucianism is a way of life. For its followers, it includes both the way they think and the way they live. Its main idea is a belief in humanity, and in the ability of normal people to constantly better themselves. One of its most influential ideas is that people's worth should be determined by their abilities. This was in contrast to previous ideas that a person's worth was determined by family status or noble blood. This led to something called a **meritocracy**, which literally meant that people should be given power based on merit and nothing else. As a result, a system emerged in China that allowed any one, no matter their class, to apply and receive government jobs. All they were required to do was pass a test and to be of male gender. Men were able to rise up to important positions in the empire, regardless of their background.

However, Confucianism eventually took over. Liu Bang also introduced the first empress to imperial China, in the form of his wife Lu Zhi. Their son, Liu Ying, was Bang's official heir, and the crown prince. Liu Bang's reign lasted until 195 B.C., when he died following an illness. Today he is known as Emperor Gaozu.

CHAPTER 4

LIFE IN THE HAN EMPIRE

The Han Dynasty established many customs and traditions. Even after the end of the Han Dynasty, many of these continued to be a part of life in China for hundreds, or even thousands, of years. From the social order, to the popularity of certain religions, the customs started during the time of the Han Empire continued through the centuries.

LEADERSHIP AND SOCIAL CLASSES

The emperor was at the absolute top of society during the Han Dynasty. He was the most powerful person in the country. He was the only person able to make new laws, or dismiss old ones. He could also **pardon** anybody of any crime. The emperor was considered so far above everyone else in society that he could not be addressed by name. To even enter the emperor's palace without permission was punishable by death. The emperor was always a member of the Liu family. This meant that all emperors were descended from Gaozu, the first ruler of the Han Dynasty.

Just below the emperor was the dowager empress. This was the wife of the previous emperor. She was also usually the mother of the current ruler. The only person with a higher rank than the dowager empress, other than the emperor, was the grand dowager empress.

Life in the Han Empire was based on the teachings of Confucius, the Chinese philosopher and teacher. According to his teachings, showing respect to parents and to elders was very important. This is one tradition that is still very much alive in many Asian countries today.

The grand dowager empress was the grandmother of the current emperor. She held the title if she was still alive when he came to power. Below the dowager empress was the empress, the emperor's wife.

Many of the emperor's male relatives were kings. They each collected taxes from a particular area. These areas were called **fiefdoms**. Female relatives like sisters and daughters were often made princesses. They also controlled fiefdoms.

Below nobles were government officials. Serving the empire by doing government work was considered one of the most honorable things a person could do. As a result, they were given a high position in society. Scholars were given a similar level of respect.

Rich nobles and government officials in China lived in luxury. Old paintings and archaeological finds show their grand lifestyle.

Emperor Wu of Han was the seventh emperor of the Han Dynasty. Under his rule, the Han Empire reached its greatest expansion. The empire reached the borders of modern Korea in the east, and Vietnam in the south.

The second social tier was made up mostly of farmers. This was considered an honorable profession, as they fed the empire. Below them, though still on the second tier, were skilled artisans and craftsmen.

The lowest social tier consisted of marketplace **merchants**, who sold their wares in shops in city markets. They had very few rights, and were forced to wear white clothes. This was done so they could be easily identified. They were not allowed to own land, and could not hold public office.

Lastly, below even merchants, were slaves. Slaves only made up about one percent of the empire's population. People could become slaves by falling into deep debt and selling themselves into it. State-owned slaves were often prisoners of war, or even family members of someone who had been convicted of a crime.

RELIGION

Confucianism became very popular during the Han Dynasty. This was very different than in the Qin Dynasty, where it was actively suppressed. The teachings of Confucius focused on harmony and respect between people. They emphasized strong family relationships. These teachings contributed to the tradition of **ancestor** worship. Although it is considered by some to be a religion, Confucianism was used more as a guiding philosophy during the Han Dynasty.

Folk religions were also popular, with different regions worshipping different gods and spirits. Heaven played an important part in Chinese belief systems. The emperor and his family were thought to be chosen by God. This concept was called the Mandate of Heaven.

In Chinese philosophy, yin and yang describe how two opposite forces, such as light and dark, often work together.

BUDDHISM IN CHINA

Buddhism came to China during the Han Dynasty in first century A.D. It made its way to the country from India. Over the years, Buddhism became an important part of Chinese culture. Later Chinese rulers adopted Buddhism as their religion.

ANCESTOR WORSHIP

The ancient Chinese believed that a person had two souls. These were called the hun and the po. After someone died, the hun would go to heaven, and live forever. The po, however, remained on earth. The po often lived in special spirit tablets. It was believed that the spirits of a person's ancestors affected the mortal world and cared about everyday affairs. Out of respect, these ancestors were prayed to and given great honor. They were also often given gifts that they might need in the afterlife. These gifts were given both at the person's funeral, and at altars in the family's home. These traditions placed a great emphasis on family relationships, with both the living and the dead.

One is always necessary for the other. In this way, two different parts are equal halves of a greater whole. This idea is at the center of much of Chinese culture.

FAMILY LIFE AND STRUCTURE

Family was very important in the Han Dynasty. Confucianism stressed good relations between family members. **Deceased** ancestors were worshipped and often asked for help in everyday affairs. Most families were made up of two parents and their children. Families also belonged to larger groups, called clans. Clans were all related through one ancestor in the male line. Members of the mother's family were not considered part of the clan, but were outside relatives.

There were four degrees of closeness in clans. The first, and most important, were brothers, and any male **descendants** of brothers. These included sons and grandsons.

Next were uncles on the father's side and all their male descendants. After that came great-uncles on the father's side, followed by great-great-uncles on the father's side, and, of course, their sons and grandsons.

During the Han Dynasty, most marriages were arranged. This meant that people didn't choose who to marry. Matches were made by parents or grandparents. There were also strict rules for when a divorce was allowed. Seven specific situations could be used as reasons for a man divorcing his wife.

SCHOOL SYSTEM

As **civil servants** became more important to the empire, so did education. Unlike in the Qin Dynasty, educated men were considered extremely valuable. The better educated a person was, the better a civil servant he would be. The most important school was the Taixue. This was a state-run school located in the capital, Chang'an. The Taixue was also linked to smaller schools around the country. The Taixue was similar to a college or university today. The curriculum was based on Confucianism. Other private schools weren't run by the state. These schools sometimes taught different meanings of Confucius's teachings from the version taught at the Taixue.

SITTING FOR THE EXAM

If a person wanted to become civil servant, they had to take the Imperial Civil Service Exam. There were no age limits, and they could take the exam as many times as they wanted. The better a person did on the tests, the higher the position they could get. The exam tested knowledge of the military, mathematics, geography, and **calligraphy**.

The Imperial Civil Service Exam was used by all future emperors. Chinese officials who passed the demanding tests wore badges that showed their rank or level in the government **hierarchy** (inset).

Regardless of where a person went to school, the goal was the same: taking the Imperial Civil Service Exam. This exam tested people on Confucian teachings. A high mark allowed a person into the civil service of the government. This was a highly respected position. This system also meant that the most qualified men actually received the best jobs. Family connections, social standing, and wealth did not matter. This also allowed men of lower social standing to rise up to important positions in the empire. This level of fairness was quite rare in the ancient world.

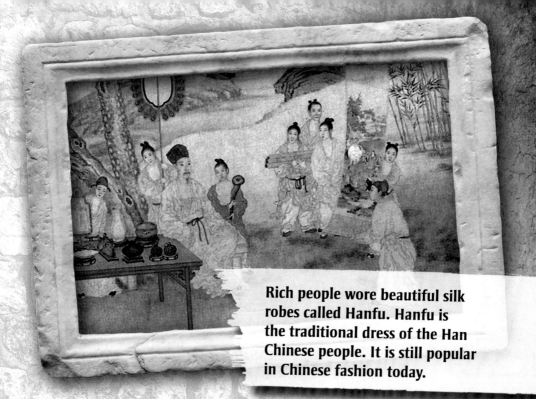

Rich people wore beautiful silk robes called Hanfu. Hanfu is the traditional dress of the Han Chinese people. It is still popular in Chinese fashion today.

LIFE IN CITIES

Life was very different for the rich and the poor in cities. The rich were able to live extravagantly. They held positions of power and influence. Many were civil servants, or were attending school so they could become one. They dressed in beautiful silks and furs. The poor wore less expensive, coarser clothing. Many poor people worked as merchants, who were looked down upon. They also lived in very different homes. The richest lived in spectacular palaces. The poor lived crammed together in smaller homes.

LIFE IN THE COUNTRY

Most people who lived in the country worked as farmers. China was built on agriculture, and farmers were respected by everyone.

Rice cultivation was especially important. Planting of rice in China started about 3,000 to 4,000 years ago. Rice became a very important part of the Chinese diet. With the development of new farming techniques during the Han Dynasty, rice farming became very important in Chinese culture and economy. Land **terraces** for planting rice and special irrigation or watering techniques were developed to harvest as much rice as possible from the available land.

Many farmers did not own the land they worked. They tended the crops for landlords, who often lived in the city. They paid these landlords half the crops they harvested. In addition to land, they received a house, as well as tools, and sometimes **livestock**. They kept the crops they didn't pay rent with. They wore homemade clothes, and were sometimes forced by the government to work on construction projects.

Well-tended rice fields layered on mountain slopes used sophisticated irrigation methods. They form spectacular patterns throughout China to this day.

CHAPTER 5

IMPACT AND LEGACY

The Han Dynasty took the foundations of the previous Qin Dynasty and built on them. They gave up the **tyranny** that marked Qin rule but kept its useful ideas. These included uniting the country, and providing the massive bureaucracy it took to run it. Both the Qin and the Han Dynasties placed the emperor at the top of their society, but those emperors ruled in very different ways.

The Han Dynasty's adoption of Confucianism influenced and shaped Chinese values all the way to the present day. Other religions like Taoism and Buddhism would eventually become popular, but Confucian teachings were already deeply planted in Chinese society. The Han government was used as the model for future dynasties, until the twentieth century.

The Han Dynasty fell in A.D. 220, after lasting for over four hundred years. Its contributions to the world are still in effect. The Silk Road, a network of trading routes that stretched all the way to the Mediterranean Sea, was started during Han rule. These routes linked together cultures from China, India, the Middle East, and even Europe.

A giant sculpture of the first Chinese emperor, Qin Shi Huang, stands near the site of his tomb in Xi'an in China.

The concept of a meritocracy was introduced by Confucius and put into practice in Han China. Today, it informs every aspect of our society. Jobs are awarded to candidates based on their abilities, instead of who they are related to or how wealthy they are. The Civil Service Exam, first implemented by the Han Dynasty, continued to be used and expanded on by later dynasties.

The imperial model of government lasted until 1912. From the time of the first Qin emperor in 221 B.C., it lasted over 2,000 years. That's an impressive amount of time for any government system to endure. In comparison, democracy was invented in ancient Athens, but the version we use today has been around only since about the seventeenth century!

Puyi, the final ruler of the Qing Dynasty, was also the last emperor of China. He was removed from power in 1912 and died in 1967 after many years of hardship.

Today, visitors can see examples of former imperial splendor in the Forbidden City in Beijing. It was the Chinese imperial palace for the Ming and Qing dynasties and was built from 1406 to 1420. It includes many influences from the Han Dynasty.

All civilizations benefited from the many Han inventions. The seismometer, a device that warns of sudden earthquakes, was invented during Han rule. More sophisticated map making, mathematical formulas that are valid to this day, and even wheelbarrows were also passed to us from the time of the Han Empire.

Even with all these contributions, one invention might be more impressive than the rest. The Han Dynasty is generally credited with inventing paper in A.D. 105. The new invention was immediately in demand, and had a huge effect on the rest of the world. Why, without the Han Dynasty and the invention of paper, you wouldn't even be reading this book!

GLOSSARY

ancestor: someone people are descended from, like a grandparent or great-grandparent

bureaucracy: a system of government with many complicated rules and ways of doing things

calligraphy: the art or profession of producing elegant writing

civil servant: a person who works in the government

civil war: a series of military actions fought by opposing groups from the same country

deceased: no longer alive; dead

descendant: a person that is born after the current generation, like a daughter or grandson

dynasty: a government where all the rulers are from the same family

elixir: a magical liquid that can extend life

feudal: a system where people work and fight for nobles who protect them and give them land

fiefdoms: large areas of land ruled by members of the nobility

fortification: a structure that is built to protect a place

hierarchy: a system divided into different levels

immortal: living forever

innovation: a new idea or method

intellectual: a thoughtful, studious person

livestock: farm animals

mausoleum: a building where dead bodies are kept

merchants: people who make a living selling goods and products

meritocracy: a system where people are chosen and move ahead based on their skill

mint: a place where coins are made

mythology: a group of related stories, often about the origin of a people

pardon: to allow a person who is guilty of a crime to go free without punishment

peasant: a farmer or laborer with low social status

terrace: a flat area on the side of a hill made for growing crops

tyranny: cruel and unfair treatment by people with power

FOR MORE INFORMATION

Books

Deady, Kathleen W., and Muriel L. Dubois. *Ancient China: Beyond the Great Wall*. North Mankato, MN: Capstone, 2011.

Demuth, Patricia Brennan. *Where Is the Great Wall?* New York, NY: Grosset & Dunlap, 2015.

O'Connor, Jane. *Hidden Army: Clay Soldiers of Ancient China*. New York, NY: Grosset & Dunlap, 2011.

Websites

Due to the changing nature of Internet links, PowerKids Press has developed an online list of websites related to the subject of this book. This site is updated regularly. Please use this link to access the list:

www.powerkidslinks.com/acc/qin

INDEX